MM's BOOK

J.S.M. Ward

LONDON

LEWIS MASONIC

Uniform with this book and by the same author

The EA's Handbook
The FC's Handbook

Tenth impression 1991

ISBN 085318 081 4
© 1991 Lewis Masonic
Terminal House, Shepperton, Middx.

Printed by Ian Allan Printing Ltd at their works
at Coombelands in Runnymede, England

PREFACE

THE third degree in Freemasonry is termed the *Sublime Degree* and the title is truly justified. Even in its exoteric aspect its simple, yet dramatic, power must leave a lasting impression on the mind of every Cand. . But its esoteric meaning contains some of the most profound spiritual instruction which it is possible to obtain to-day.

Even the average man, who entered The Craft with little realisation of its real antiquity and elaborate symbolism, cannot fail to be impressed with the solemnity of this, its greatest degree. In its directness and apparent simplicity rests its tremendous power. The exoteric and esoteric are interwoven in such a wonderful way that it is almost impossible to separate the one from the other, and the longer it is studied the more we realise the profound and ancient wisdom concealed therein. Indeed, it is probable that we shall never master all that lies hidden in this degree till we in very truth pass through that reality of which it is an allegory.

The two degrees which have gone before, great and beautiful though they be, are but the training and preparation for the message which the third degree holds in almost every line of the ritual. Here at length we learn the true purpose of Freemasonry. It is not merely a system of morality, veiled in allegory and illustrated by symbols, but a great adventure, a search after that which was lost; in other words, the Mystic Quest, the craving of the Soul to comprehend the nature of God and to achieve union with Him.

Different men vary greatly; to some the most profound teachings appeal, while to others simpler and more direct instruction is all they crave. But there is hardly a man who has not, at some time or other, amid the turmoil and distraction of this material world, felt a strange and unaccountable longing for knowledge as to why he was ever sent here, whence he came, and whither he is wending. At such times he feels like a wanderer in a strange land, who has almost forgotten his native country, because he left it so long ago, but yet vaguely realises that he is an exile, and dimly craves for some message from that home which he knew of yore.

This is the voice of the Divine Spark in man calling out for union with the Source of its being, and at such times the third degree carries with it a message which till then, perhaps, the brother had not realised. The true s....ts are lost, but we are told how and where we shall find them. The gateway of d. opens the way to the p. within the c., where the longing spirit will find peace in the arms of the Father of All.

Thus it will be seen that the third degree strikes a more solemn note than even that of d. itself, and I have endeavoured in this little book to convey in outline some part at least of this sublime message.

As in my previous books, I freely confess that I have not covered the whole ground. Not only would it be impossible to do so in a book of this size, but in so doing I should have defeated one of my principal objects in writing, namely, to inspire others to study for themselves and endeavour to find in our ceremonies further and deeper meanings.

The success of the earlier books shows clearly that my efforts have not been in vain, and that the brethren are more than anxious to fathom the inner meaning of the ceremonies we all love so well. This book completes the series dealing with the meaning of the three craft degrees, but their popularity has convinced me that the experiment of producing a small and inexpensive handbook has been completely justified. I have therefore been encouraged to write further volumes, and the next of the series will be an outline history of Freemasonry " from time Immemorial."

PREFACE TO SECOND EDITION

The success of the first edition of this book has necessitated a second wherein I have corrected a few printing errors and added a few points which may help my brother students.

From the number of letters I have received from all parts of the world, thanking me for the light these books throw on the meaning of our ceremonies, it is clear that the new members who are entering our Order are tending to take an increasing interest in the meaning of our Rites and are no longer content to regard the Ceremonies merely as a pastime for an idle hour.   J. S. M. WARD.

CONTENTS

Introduction by The Hon. Sir John Cockburn,
M.D., K.C.M.G., P.G.D.Eng.,
P.D.G.M. S. Australia

INTRODUCTION

By Sir John A. Cockburn,

W. Bro. Ward has lost no time in supplying his large circle of readers with this little book on the 3°. With becoming reverence he touches on the last great lesson which Masonry presents to the mind of the Craftsman. Among the manifold blessings that Freemasonry has conferred on mankind none is greater than that of taking the sting from death and robbing the grave of victory. No man can be called Free who lives in dread of the only event that is certain in his life. Until emancipated from the fear of death, he is all his life long subject to bondage. Yet how miserably weak is this phantom king of Terrors who enslaves so many of the uninitiated. As Francis Bacon remarked, there is no passion in the mind of man that does not master the dread of death. Revenge triumphs over it; love slights it; honour aspireth to it; grief flieth to it. Death has always been regarded as the elucidation of the Great Mystery. It was only at the promise of dissolution that the seeker after the Elixir of Life exclaimed *Eureka*. Masonry regards death but as the gate of life, and the Master Mason learns to look forward with firm but humble confidence to the moment when he will receive his summons to ascend to the Grand Lodge above.

Brother Ward very properly attaches much significance to the Pass Word leading to the 2° and 3°. In the Eleusinian Mysteries an ear of corn was presented to the Epoptai. This, as an emblem of Ceres, represented by the S.W., is appropriate to the F.C.'s, who are under the guidance of that officer, while the name of the first artificier in metals, which is reminiscent of Vulcan, the Celestial Blacksmith, seems specially befitting to the attributes of the J.W., as it was in the days before 1740. The author sees in the lozenge formed by two of the great lights a representation of the Vesica Piscis. This symbol, whose literal meaning is " the bladder of the fish," is of deep significance. Some see in it the essential scheme of ecclesiastical architecture. But as the spiritually blind are unable to discern similitudes, so those who are gifted with deep insight are apt to over estimate analogies. The Vesica Piscis being, as Brother Ward rightly states, a feminine emblem, and therefore one sided, can hardly represent the equilibrium attained by the conjunction of the square and compasses. These respectively stand for the contrasted correlatives which pervade Creation, and, like the pillars, are typical when conjoined of new stability resulting from their due proportion in the various stages of Evolution. The progressive disclosures of the points of the compasses seems to indicate the ultimate realisation of the spirituality of matter ; the at-one-ment and reconciliation at which Freemasonry and all true religions aim. Brother Ward repeatedly points out the similarity that exists between the lessons of Christianity and of Freemasonry. It is indeed difficult to distinguish between them. The Ancient Mysteries undoubtedly possessed in secret many of the truths proclaimed in the gospel. St. Augustine affirms that Christianity, although not previously known by that name, had always existed. But whereas the hope of immortality was formerly in the Mysteries confined to a favoured few, the new Convenant opened the Kingdom of Heaven to all believers. Incidentally this little volume clears up many passages which are obscure in the Ritual. For example, there could be no object in directing that the F.C's, who, on account of their trust-worthiness, were selected by the King to search for the Master, should be clothed in white to prove their innocence. That was already beyond question. The order was evidently meant for the repentant twelve who took no actual part in the crime. This and similar inconsistencies in the Ritual may be accepted as evidence of its antiquity. Had it been a modern compilation such contradictions would have been studiously avoided.

It is probable that many earnest Masons may not agree with all Brother Ward's interpretations. Nor can such unanimity reasonably be expected. Freemasonry, as a gradual accretion of the Wisdom of Ages Immemorial, bears traces of many successive schools of thought. But all its messages are fraught with hope for the regeneration of humanity. The author intimated his desire in this series of handbooks to lead others to prosecute the study of Masonry for themselves ; and indeed he has abundantly proved that in its unfathomable depths there are many gems of priceless ray serene which

will well repay the search.   Brother Ward is heartily
to be congratulated on having attained the object
he had in view.

JOHN A. COCKBURN.

CHAPTER I

QUESTIONS AND P.W.

Those of our Brethren who have read the previous two books of this series will not need much help in understanding the significance of the questions which are put to the Cand. before being raised. Practically every question has been dealt with in detail in the previous books ; the majority of them are taken from incidents in the Lectures and Tracing Board, and since the latter was explained at some length we shall not now detain our readers long.

The manner of preparation for the second degree stressed the masculine side, which is characteristic of it. The admission on a S. indicated that the Cand. had profited by the moral training received in the First degree, and that his conduct had always been on the S. . There is, however, a deep esoteric meaning in the apparent platitude that it is the fourth part of a circle. Among all the ancient nations the circle is a symbol of God the Infinite, Whose name we discovered in the second degree in the M.Ch., where we learnt that it consisted of four letters. Thus the Cand. was admitted on one letter of the Mystic Name, and if the four Sq.s are united with the circle in a peculiar way they form the cosmic cross, emblem of matter, within the circle of the Infinite.

We have in the last book considered at such length what is implied by the words " Hidden mysteries of nature and science," that we need here only refer our readers to that section, wherein we saw that in former times these hidden mysteries undoubtedly referred to certain occult powers, which would be dangerous if acquired by a man who had not proved himself to be of the highest moral character.

The " wages " we receive consist of the power to comprehend the nature of God, Who resides in the M.Ch. of the Soul of every Mason. The F.C. receives his wages without scruple or diffidence because the Spiritual benefit he receives from Freemasonry is in exact proportion to his desire, and ability, to comprehend its inner meaning.

He cannot receive either more or less than he has earned, for if he has not understood the profound lesson of the Divinity within him, naturally he cannot benefit therefrom.

His employers are the Divine Trinity, of Whom Justice is one of the outstanding attributes. God could not be unjust and remain God. This conception is almost a platitude, but the average man, while realising that God will not withhold any reward earned, is at times apt to assume that because God is love He will reward us more than we deserve. This is clearly a mistake, for God could not be partial without ceasing to be God, therefore the F.C. receives exactly the Spiritual wages he has earned, and neither more nor less, but some F.C.'s will nevertheless obtain a greater reward than others, because spiritually they have earned it.

The significance of the names of the P....rs was explained in the last book, but in view of the nature of the third degree it seems advisable to point out once more that their secret Kabalistic meaning is (1) Being fortified by every moral virtue, (2) you are now properly prepared, (3) to undergo that last and greatest trial which fits you to become a M M. . Thus we see that even the w....ds of the preceding degrees lead up to this, the last and greatest.

3

As in the former case, the remark of the W.M. that he will put other questions if desired indicates the possibility of members of the Lodge asking questions based on the Lectures of the Second Degree, or even on the Tracing Board. It is, indeed, a pity that this right is practically never exercised. For example, a particularly appropriate question would be " What was the name of the man who cast the two great p....rs ? " As it is, the Cand. in a dramatic way represents the closing incidents in the life of this great man, whose importance till then he has hardly had any opportunity of realising.

Having answered these test questions, the cand. is again entrusted with a P.W., etc., to enable him to enter the Lodge after it has been raised to the Third degree during this temporary absence. We have in the previous book explained that the raising of a Lodge should alter the vibrations of those present by a process well recognised in the ceremonies of Magic, and, to enable the Cand. quickly to become in tune with these higher spiritual vibrations, a word of " power " is given him, which in a moment places him on the same plane as the other members of the Lodge. This word he has to give,

4

not only outside the d....r of the Lodge, but also immediately before his presentation by the S.W. as " Properly prepared to be raised to the Third Degree." It is only after this has been done that the real ceremony of the Third Degree, so far as the C. is concerned, begins, and therefore that the full force of the vibrations of the M.M.'s come into play.

The P.W. itself is of the greatest significance, more especially when combined with the P.W. leading from the First to the Second degree. At one time the P.W.'s were reversed. T.C. being the W. leading to the Second, and Sh..... the W. leading to the Third. This is still the case in those foreign Grand Lodges, such as the Dutch and the French, which derive from us before 1740, when the W.s were altered owing to certain un-authorised revelations. This alteration was one of the just grievances which brought about the secession of the so-called " Ancients," who charged Grand Lodge with altering the Ancient Landmarks. When the Irish followed our example they continued the prohibition of the introduction of m....ls until the Third degree, which is a logical procedure, for clearly you have no right to bring them into Lodge until you have been symbolically introduced to the first artificer in that material.   As the W.s now stand they convey the following spiritual lesson :—the F.C. is one who finds the simple necessities of life, such as C. and W., sufficient for his requirements. They are plenty to the spiritually minded man, whose soul becomes clogged and hampered by the acquisition of worldly possessions, and since it is hard for a rich man to enter the Kingdom of Heaven, immediately the Cand. has symbolically received W.P. he is Sl....n.

T.C. conveys the lesson that W.P. in themselves bring death to the soul and prevent its upward progress.   To-day, the river of death connected with the P.W. leading to the Second degree has largely lost its significance, whereas when it was a P.W. leading to the Third, it was in itself a fine allegory.

We must remember that Bunyan's *Pilgrim's Progress* was well known and widely read at the beginning of the 18th Century, and those who were re-organising our rituals at that time could not have been blind to the similarity of the allegory hidden in the w. Sh. and the account by Bunyan of Christian's fording the river of death on the way

6

to the Holy City. The change of about 1740 destroyed this allegory, and its survival in the Tracing Board is now merely one of those numerous footmarks which, to the careful student, are invaluable indications of the various transformations through which our ritual has passed during the course of years. Nevertheless, I do not regret the change, as I think the present spiritual lesson is even finer than the former one, but the other arrangement was more logical. Firstly, from the practical point of view the F.C. required the use of m...l tools to perform his operative tasks, and in the process of his work acquired W.P., in contradiction to the E.A., who did only rough work and received only maintenance : i.e., corn, wine, and oil. Secondly, from the symbolical standpoint the sequence was also more logical, for the F.C., having acquired wealth by means of his skill, was brought to the river of d., and passed through it in the Third Degree.

According to Bro. Sanderson, in his " Examination of the Masonic Ritual," the actual translation of the Hebrew w. Sh. is an " e. of c., or a f. of w."— hence the manner in which it is depicted in a F.C.'s Lodge—while the w. T.C. in Hebrew means only a

7

blacksmith, though another w. similarly pronounced means *acquisition*. Hence, as he points out, " an allegorical title has, in translating the Old Testament, been mistaken for the name of an actual person, for the name itself means ' A worker in M....t....ls ' " Therefore the connection with H.A.B. is obvious. Bro. Sanderson, quoting from the " Secret Discipline," by S. L. Knapp, says, " In a work on ancient ecclesiastical history the following occurs, ' By a singular *plasus linguae* the moderns have substituted T.C. in the Third Degree for *tymboxein*— to be entombed.' " While I am unable to say whether Knapp is justified in this statement, it is quite probable that this P.W., and indeed all the P.W.s are comparatively modern substitutes, taken from the Bible to replace ancient W.s of power whose full meaning was lost and whose form in consequence had become corrupt and unintelligible. The Greek word *tymboxein* would be peculiarly suitable for a P.W. leading to the Third Degree, in view of its meaning, and mediaeval magical ceremonies are full of corrupt Greek words indiscriminately mingled with equally corrupt Hebrew and Arabic. There is, therefore, nothing intrinsically improbable in the suggestion that this ancient Greek word was the original from which T.C. has been

8

evolved. We know as a fact that large pieces of Biblical history were imported wholesale into our rituals in the 18th Century, and what is more likely than that an unintelligible work, already so corrupt as not even to be recognisable as Greek, should be amended into a well known Biblical character? However, the word as it stands, because of its Hebrew meaning of acquisition, can correctly be translated as W.P., while as meaning an artificer in M. it clearly refers to H.A.B., who made the two p......rs, and whom the Cand. is to represent. Thus, following this line of interpretation, we perceive that the Cand. really represents H.A.B. when he enters the Lodge, although under the disguised title conveyed by the P.W..

In dealing with these P.W.s I have endeavoured to show that there are meanings within meanings, and the same is true of practically every important incident in the whole ceremony. In a book of this size it is obviously impossible to attempt to give all of these meanings, and even if one did the result would be to befog the young reader and so prevent him from getting a clear and connected interpretation of the ceremony. It is for this reason that, in the main, I am concentrating on one line of interpretation, but I have thought it desirable in this section to give a hint to more advanced students, so that they can follow up similar lines of investigation for themselves.

PREPARATION

In English and Scotch workings there is no c.t. around the Cand. in preparation for the Third Degree, but in the Irish working it is wound once around his n., in the Second degree twice, and the First three times. If we regard the c.t. as symbolising those things which hamper a man's spiritual progress, the gradual unwinding of it as used in Irish workings becomes of great significance. This interpretation implies that the Cand. is hampered in Body, Soul and Spirit in the First Degree, whereas by the time he has reached this point in the Third Degree the Body and Soul have triumphed over the sins which peculiarly assail them, and in that stage symbolised by the Degree itself the Spirit has only to triumph over Spiritual sins, such as Spiritual Pride. With this exception the manner of preparation is the same in all these British workings, and indicates that the Cand. is now about to consecrate both sides of his nature, active and passive, creative and preservative, etc., to the service of the Most High.

The explanation already given in the previous books of the various details, such as being s.s., holds here, and a brief glance at the other volumes will render it unnecessary for me to take up valuable space therewith in this third book. The Can. is then brought to the Lodge door and gives the Kn.s of a F.C. These Kn's indicate that Soul and Body are in union, but the Spirit is still out of contact, whereas the proper Kn's of a M.M. (2/1) indicate that the Spirit dominates the Soul and is in union with it, the body having fallen away into significance. It will be remembered that in the first book of this series I pointed out that the three separate kn's of an E.A. symbolise that in the uninitiated man, Body, Soul and Spirit are all at variance. Meanwhile the Lodge has been raised to a Third Degree by a ceremony whose profound significance demands consideration in a separate chapter.

CHAPTER II

THE OPENING

Having satisfied himself that all present are symbolically upright and moral men, the W.M. asks the J.W. if his spiritual nature has evolved sufficiently to control both soul and body. The J.W. suggests that he should be tested, not only by the emblem of upright conduct, but also by the Compasses. Now these combined with the Square form a lozenge, which is itself a symbol for the Vesica Piscis, emblem of the female principle. The Compasses, moreover, are the instruments with which geometrical figures are created, and more especially the Circle. By means of two circles the triangle, emblem of the triune nature of God, is produced, while the Circle itself is the emblem of Eternity and therefore of Spirit. A point within the circle forms the symbol for the Hindu conception of the Supreme Being, Paramatma, whence we have come and whither we shall all ultimately return. At the centre of the circle rests all knowledge ; there shall we find every lost secret. Now such a figure

12

can only be drawn with the help of the Compasses, and in drawing it the following significant symbolical act takes place.

One point of the Compass rests at the centre, and the other makes the circle of the Infinite. No matter how far the legs of the Compass be extended, or how large the Circle, the fact remains that one leg is always at the centre. Thus the Compasses, while they travel through infinity, are at the same time never separated from the centre, and from that point cannot err.

This instrument may therefore be considered as standing for the Divine Spark in Man, in all its manifestations. One of these is conscience ; but the Divine Spark has many attributes and names.

So the J.W.'s reply indicates that he is prepared to be tested both by the moral code and by the spiritual laws of our being.

But after these preliminaries the proceedings become of an even more exalted nature. All that has gone before has been but preparation for the Great Quest on which we must now set forth. It is the quest of the Soul for realisation of God, and at-one-ment with Him. This is the Mystic Quest of all ages, and, true to the ancient symbolism, it starts from the East, the place of Light, and goes towards the West, the place of darkness and death.

The East represents God, Who is our home. It indicates that each soul comes out from the place of Light, from Light itself, that is, from the very substance of God, descends through the Gateway of the Dawn and becomes incarnate in Matter. But it brings with it a sense of loss and separation, for it has come out from God, and the Divine Spark within it longs to return whence it came. Having lost the secret of its true nature and the way of return, it wanders in darkness, seeking, and for most men the way of return is through the Western portal, the gateway of Death, for so long as we are finite beings we cannot hope to comprehend the Infinite.

Yet there are some few exceptions to the general rule, who, while still in the flesh, have a vision of the Divine splendour, are caught up in it, and become one with God. To such men the return to ordinary mundane existence seems unreal and shadowy. Where others believe in God they *Know* Him, but it is almost impossible for them to convey to others the experience through which they have gone. Yet that such experiences are real, as real as any other fact in life, is attested by a long line of witnesses right throughout the ages.

To the average man, however, the first real step towards the realisation of what constitutes God is through the portal of physical death;—but even then the end is still far off.

Hence the answer explaining how the true secrets came to be lost indicates, not the cause of the loss, but the first step towards the recovery, and this fact is borne out by the subsequent events in the ceremony itself.

Note, it is the body only that dies, and by its death enables the Soul and Spirit to re-discover in part the secrets which were lost. Yet this death of the Body effectually debars the communication of these secrets to the sorrowing F.C.'s left behind. It is the passing through that veil which separates life and death which starts us on the road which ends with God.

15

It must never be forgotten, however, that the genuine secrets are never recovered in the Craft, although symbolically we rise from the grave, for that secret can only be discovered at or with the C.—i.e., with God. To that *exalted* position we can only attain after long journeys through the planes of existence beyond the grave. In our symbolism there is nothing which indicates that immediately after death man is fit to pass into the presence of the King of Kings.

But the Divine Spark within us is never really separated from the Great and All-Pervading Spirit. It is still part of it, though its glory is dimmed by the veil of flesh. Therefore, just as one arm of the compasses ever rests on the centre, no matter how far the other leg travels, so however far we may travel from God, and however long and hard may be the journey, the Divine Spark within us can never be truly separated from Him, or err from that Centre. Thus the point of the Compasses at the centre of the circle may be considered to be the Spirit, the head of the Compasses the Soul, and the point on the circumference the body.

So the task is set and the brethren go forth on the quest, that quest which must lead through the darkness of death, as the ceremony that follows tells in allegory. It is not correct to say that the search hinted at in the Opening ceremony is suddenly abandoned, and those who think this misinterpret the whole meaning of the legend. Never in earthly life shall we find the answer we seek, nay, even death itself will not give it ; but, having passed beyond the grave, through the four veils of the Scottish rite, and so into the H.R.A., we find an *excellent* answer in allegorical and symbolical language, whilst the jewel of the degree emphasises what the end of the quest is.

Nor must it be forgotten that the body alone cannot realise the nature of God, and that is why without the help of the other two, H.A.B. neither *could*, nor would, disclose the S........t.

The W.M.'s promise to help indicates that the Spirit will render assistance, but though the Spirit subsequently raises man from the grave it is not sufficiently evolved to give him the true secret. This can only come about when the Spirit has raised the Soul to a far higher stage of spirituality.

Though this is the degree of Destruction, that form of the Trinity is not invoked, and the title used corresponds more closely to the Hindu name for the All-Embracing than to their form of the Destroyer. This no doubt is deliberate, for the symbol of this degree is the same emblem which among the Hindus denotes the Most High, namely the Circle with a Point within it.

In some Scotch rituals, after the Lodge has been opened in the first degree the I.P.M., or the D.C., opens the V.S.L., and, strange to say, does so with the words, " In the beginning was the Word." Similarly, when the Lodge is closed in the first degree the book is closed with the words, " And the Word was with God." Here then we get two striking features : (1) the use of words from the first chapter of the Gospel according to St. John, and (2) their correlation with the phrase in the Third Degree, " At, or with the C." This procedure suggests that the lost W. is the Logos, or Christ, and remembering what we have previously pointed out in the earlier books, i.e., that there is a perfectly logical Christian interpretation of the whole of the Craft ceremonies, this fact becomes of increasing significance.

Before closing this chapter, I would like to add that the Third Degree lends itself to a Christian interpretation even more markedly than the former ones, and several of the higher degrees in Freemasonry adopt and expand this line of teaching.

In view of the fact that in the Middle Ages Freemasonry was undoubtedly Christian, we cannot lightly reject this view of the inner meaning of the ceremonies, but as the frame work of our ceremonies apparently goes back before Christian times, a non-Christian interpretation is equally permissible.

CHAPTER III

THE SYMBOLICAL JOURNEYS, ETC.

The Can. is admitted on he C.......s, and this fact is of far greater significance than most brethren probably realise. Firstly, as has been noted, one arm of the C.s is always at the C., no matter how far the other may travel, and from the point of view of the Can., though he knows it not, this act in a sense indicates that his heart, and therefore he himself, is at or on the C.......e. Secondly, the C.......s in this degree link up with the Sq. used in the former degree on a similar occasion. We have seen in the previous books that the Sq. and C.......s are united on the Ped. in such a way as to form the vesica piscis, the emblem of the female principle, and the symbol of birth and rebirth. Hence symbolically the Can. passes through the vesica piscis. Also after entering the Lodge in this, as in the previous degrees, he kn......s while the blessing of Heaven is invoked, and as he does so the wands of the deacons are crossed above his head. He thus kn.......s in a triangle, the emblem of Spirit, and itself connected with the lozenge. Two equilateral triangles make a lozenge, which is produced from the vesica piscis—formed by two circles, as shown by the first proposition in Euclid. In view of the great stress laid upon Geometry throughout the whole of our rituals these facts cannot be ignored. Our Operative Brn. must have realised that the whole science of Geometry arises out of this first proposition, which shows how to make a triangle (the emblem of the Trinity and the Spirit) by means of two circles whose circumferences pass through the centre of each other. In doing so they form the vesica piscis, which gives birth first of all to the triangle, and secondly, to the double triangle, in the form of a lozenge. This last emblem is symbolised by the sq., denoting matter, and the c...s, denoting spirit. The above facts throw a flood of light upon the interplay between these Masonic emblems.

Before leaving this subject it is worth while pointing out that the Can. likewise takes every Ob. in Craft masonry within this triangle, and that the same method is employed in other ancient rites, including those of the Society of Heaven and Earth in China, where the Can. kn...s on one sword, while two others are held over his head so as to form a triangle of steel.

The Can. now starts on his three symbolical journeys. He first satisfies the J.W., representing the Body, that he is an E.A., i.e., a man of good moral character. He next satisfies the S.W., representing the Soul, that he has benefited by the lessons of life and acquired intellectual knowledge. Then comes the third journey, when he is once more challenged by the Soul, who demands the P.W., the full significance of which has already been explained. Let us combine these meanings ! He comes laden with worldly possessions, which in themselves carry the seeds of death, unconsciously representing in his person the worker in metals who made the twin columns, and is about to be entombed. (tymboxein).

Therefore the Soul presents him to the Spirit as one properly prepared to carry out the part of his great predecessor. There is a point here which we need to realise, for it is one which is often overlooked. In the previous degrees only one Deacon was instructed to lead the Can. by the proper S....ps to the E., but here both are needed. From the practical point of view there is no obvious reason why the help of the J.D. should be invoked at all, and as the ceremony is usually carried out he does nothing but look on. I believe, however, the S.D.

should first go through the S....ps and the J.D. should assist the Can. to copy his example. If this were so we should get an almost exact repetition of the analogous ceremony in the R.A. where the P.S., corresponding to the S.D., is helped by an assistant. Thus, with the Can., in both cases we get a Trinity, only one of whom actually descends into the g., or, in the other case, into the v. .

As Major Sanderson has pointed out in *An Examination of the Masonic Ritual*, among the primitive races usually, a man who stepped over an o.g. would be considered to have committed sacrilege, and almost certainly would be slain, but, on the other hand, we do know that in many Initiatory Rites either the Can., or someone else for him, steps down into a gr., and is subsequently symbolically sl...n therein. If this be the true interpretation of this part of the ceremony, the reason for the presence of the two deacons in addition to the Can. becomes clear. It is only the Body that descends into the gr., the Soul and the Spirit have no part therein. Thus, for the moment, though only temporarily, these three represent the triune nature of man, while the three principal officers represent the triune nature of God. The fact that this is undoubtedly true in the case of the R.A., makes it almost certain that the same idea underlies this apparently unimportant difference between the arrangements in the third degree, and those followed in the first and second.

Again and again when one comes to study carefully the details of our ritual, one finds little points, such as these, which would certainly not have survived the drastic revision of 1816 if there had not been present some men who really did understand the inner meaning of our ceremonies, and refused to allow important lessons to be lost by the removal of what, at first sight, appear to be unnecessary details.

Therefore, those of us who value the inner meaning of our ceremonies owe a deep debt of gratitude to these men, even though their actual names be unknown to us, and on our part a duty is imposed on us that we shall not hastily tamper with the rituals, merely because we do not ourselves see the full significance of a phrase, or think that by revising it we can make the wording run more smoothly.

The next factor we must consider most carefully is the actual sp... s themselves. These make the Latin cross of suffering and sacrifice.

Sometimes the sp....s are not done quite correctly, for the Can. should be careful to face due North, due South, and due East respectively. This procedure undoubtedly refers to the three entrances of the Temple through which H.A.B. endeavoured to escape. Hence it is we see that the Master himself trod out the cross of Calvary during the tragedy, and in a sense made the Consecration Cross of the Temple.

In a mediaeval church, and even to-day at the consecration of a church according to the Anglican ordinance, there should be a dedication cross marked on the building. In the Middle Ages these were usually marked on the pillars, and apparently corresponded to the mark made by an illiterate person when witnessing a deed. The Consecrating Bishop sometimes drew this cross on the pillar or wall, or sometimes merely traced over a cross already painted there for the purpose. Any new piece of work in a church, even if only a new fresco, had its dedication cross. For example :—At Chaldon Church, Surrey, the dedication cross is marked on the margin of a fresco depicting *The Brig of Dread*, described at length in *Freemasonry and the Ancient Gods*.

Bearing these facts in mind, we shall perceive that, even from the Operative point of view, the manner of advancing in this degree, and the manner in which H.A.B. met his end, had a peculiar significance. The Great Architect of the Temple must have traced the dedication cross the whole length and breadth of the Temple in his own blood. Moreover, such dedication crosses as have actually survived are nearly always found to be painted in red. Thus, H.A.B.'s last work was, as it were, to commence the consecration of the Temple which was completed by K.S., for until that cross had been marked either on the wall or pavement, according to mediaeval Operative ideas the building could not be consecrated. Therefore, the Can., who is re-enacting the same drama, must obviously do likewise, and in so doing dedicates the Temple of his body.

But there is still more hidden within this ceremonial act. The ancient Knights Templar were accused of trampling on the cr., and a careful examination of the evidence taken at the trial shows that in reality they took a ritual sp., somewhat similar to those taken by the Can. in this degree.

One of the esoteric meanings indicated is the Way of the Cross which leads to Calvary. Furthermore, having thus traced out a cr. he is subsequently laid on it, and this fact is emphasised by the position in which his legs or feet are placed. The foot of this cr. reaches to the Ped., on which rests the O.T. If, therefore, this symbolical cr. were raised as it was on Calvary it would rest on the O.T., and the Can. would face the E., and would be, as it were, on a mountain. This fact should be borne in mind by those who seek a Christian interpretation of our Craft ceremonies. Mystically interpreted, it indicates that every aspirant for union with the Divine must tread the Way of the Cross, and suffer and die thereon, in order that he may rise to a new life, a realisation of his union with the Infinite.

Even those who are disinclined to admit the possibility of a Christian interpretation of the Craft degrees, must recognise the fact that this cr. is the cr. of sacrifice and means that the true aspirant must be prepared to sacrifice everything in his search after Truth.

The number of the sp....s is the combination of the Trinity and of the four elements, representing matter. It is the same number as forms the perfect lodge, and also the seven elements which form man, whether we interpret it according to the ancient Egyptian system, or in the more modern form of the five physical senses, the Soul and the Spirit. In the latter case it indicates that the man must be prepared to sacrifice, or shall we say dedicate to God, Body, Soul and Spirit.

There are yet other profound meanings in this one ritual act, but enough has been written to set my readers pondering for themselves, and we will therefore proceed to consider the next point in the ceremony.

The Ob. itself contains one or two interesting points. Thus it indicates that a M.M.'s Lodge must always be open on the C. . This shows us at once that we are dealing with a ceremony with a mystical meaning, for the C. means the same as the middle ch. in the second degree—the secret chamber of the heart, where dwells the Divine Spark—and so tells us in veiled language that all that happens thereafter is a spiritual experience, which sooner or later comes to every mystic. The special moral obligations which the Can. undertakes should be noted, but require no explanation. It is, however, difficult to understand why they should be deferred until this stage. In the ancient charges similar obligations are imposed apparently on the E.A., and this seems more logical.

The Py. varies even in different parts of England, but in essentials is always the same. You are s. at the c., and the manner of disposal is very reminiscent of the way in which the dead are cremated in India in honour of Shiva. There the corpse is burnt near running water, preferably near the Ganges, and the ashes are thrown into the air over the river to the four cardinal points, that the winds may scatter them. It must be remembered that Shiva represents the destructive attribute of the Deity and he makes the P.S. of a M.M. on his statues. His is the element of fire, and all these facts must be born in mind when considering our own Py.

The position of the Sq. and Cs., in addition to the explanation given, indicates that the spirit, represented by the Cs., now dominates the body, typified by the Sq. .

CHAPTER IV

THE EXHORTATION

The opening part of the exhortation gives a convenient summary of the previous degrees, and quite clearly indicates that the first inner meaning of the series is Birth, Life, which is of course educational and preparatory for its sequel, and Death. The phrase relating to the second degree " And to trace it, from its development, through the paths of Heavenly Science, even to the throne of God Himself," shows plainly its real significance. As pointed out in the F.C. Handbook, in the Mid. Ch. the F.C. discovers, not only the name of God, but that he himself is the fifth letter *Shin* which transforms the name *Jehovah* into the name *Jeheshue*, or *Messias*, the *King*.

But according to the old Kabala *Jeheshue* must be raised on the cross of *Tipareth*, and the significance of this fact is impressed on our Can. by the incidents now to take place. The average Christian need not trouble about the subtleties of the Kabala, for the story in the New Testament supplies him with a very similar interpretation.

The W.M. having, almost casually, given him this key to the inner meaning of what is about to follow, proceeds at once to the most dramatic part of the ceremony. Up to this point almost all forms of our ritual are practically the same, but henceforward there are many marked differences. " Emulation " ritual may be regarded as containing the bare minimum, but the additional details found in many Provincial workings in England, and in Scotland, Ireland, America, and many of the Continental Lodges, are too important to be ignored. There is no reason to assume that they are innovations; on the contrary all the evidence points to the fact that they are integral parts of the ceremony which, for various reasons, were omitted by the revisers of our ritual who met in the Lodge of Reconciliation. I shall therefore proceed to note and explain them where necessary.

Whereas in Emulation working as soon as the Ws. are called on the deacons retire, in most others, in the Provinces, etc., they fall back to the head of the g.. Thus with the W.M. the W.s form the triangle of Spirit, and with the D.s the Sq. of matter, on which the triangle rests, for the M. descends from his chair and stands in front of the Ped.. As a practical piece of advice I would recommend that the J.W. should not direct the Can. to c. his f. until after the S.W. has dealt with him, for it is impossible for him to drop on his respective k....s if his f. are c., whereas by carrying out these instructions before the last attack he will fall the more readily.

In most of the old Scotch rituals the Can. journeys round the Lodge, is attacked by the J.W. in the S., by the S.W. in the W. (note that), and returns to the M. in the E., where the final incident takes place. I think, however, our English system of having the attack in the N. instead of in the W. is preferable, and is probably the correct form. In the Scotch ritual the three villains have names, and the same is the case in America. They are *Jubela*, *Jubelo*, and *Jubelum*. The word itself clearly comes from the Latin word meaning " To command," and refers to the fact that they commanded him to give up the S....s. But the terminations of the three names appear to have a curious esoteric reference to India. It can hardly be by accident that these three names form the mystic word AUM. The U in India in this case is pronounced almost like O, and when this word is disguised, as it usually is, it is written OMN. If this be so we have the Creative Preservative, and

Annihilative aspects of the Deity emphasised in the Third Degree, and it is the Destructive aspect, symbolised by the letter M, which deals the final stroke.

This variation is therefore of importance, but I must warn my readers that not all Scotch workings have it, some of them being much more akin to our own, even having the attack in the N. . Practically all of them, however, have the perambulations, during which solemn music is played. The usual procedure is for the brethren to pass round the gr. once making the P.S. of an E.A. . When this is done the J.W. makes his abortive attempt. The second round is made with the H.S. of an F.C., after which the S.W. tries and fails. The third round is made with the S. of G. and D. of a M.M., on the conclusion of which the Can. is r.... by the lion's g.... It is a great pity that the use of this name for the M.M.'s g. is falling into disuse in London, for it has in itself important symbolical references, to which we shall refer later in the chapter.

In many parts of England it is still customary to place the Can., either in a c....n or in a g. made in the floor, and the same method is found in most other parts of the world. Indeed, in the Dutch ritual the Can. is first of all shown a c....n in which is a human skeleton. This is subsequently removed, though he does not know it and he thinks when he is laid therein he will find himself in its bony clutches. Even as near London as Windsor there is a Masonic Temple which has a special chamber of d. with a g. actually in the floor and until recently it was still used although whether it is to-day I cannot say.

Let us now turn to consider the meanings of the main incidents. The first meaning of the degree is obvious; it prepares a man for his final end and hints of a possibility of life beyond the grave but it must be admitted that the lesson is not driven home with the same force as it is in most of the ancient mysteries. Osiris Himself rose from the dead and became the Judge of all who followed after Him, and because of this fact His worshippers believed that they too would rise. In our legend, however, it is only the dead body of H.A.B. which is lifted out of the g. in a peculiar manner, and in the legend there is not even a hint as to what befell his Soul. The question is often asked why they should have raised a c....s and placed it on its feet.[1]

---

[1] See Ward, *Who Was Hiram Abiff?*

One explanation probably is, by analogy with the Greek story of the manner in which Hercules recovered Alcestis and ransomed her from the bondage of *Thanatos*—Death himself. We are told that Hercules wrestled with Thanatos and would not let him go until he had agreed to allow Hercules to bring her back from the realm of the Shades to the land of living men. It may be that the corpse here represents Death. It is also worth noting that Isis joined together the fragments of the body of Osiris, and the " Setting up " of the backbone of the God was a ceremony carried out every year by the ancient Egyptian Priests. The body of Osiris apparently was raised from the bier by Anubis in precisely the same way as the M.M. is r........ When it was set on its feet life returned to it. One fact is certain, that in every Rite which has as its central theme symbolic d. the Can. is r. by the same g., and in precisely the same manner, and this manner becomes a method of greeting and of recognition among all who have passed through this type of ceremony. For example :—it is known and used in the Dervish Rite, among West African Negroes, among the Red Indians of Central America, and was apparently known to the ancient Druids, for it is carved on a stone found at Iona. In the ancient rites of Mithra it also appears to have been the method used upon a similar occasion. These facts show that it is an ancient landmark and one to be most carefully guarded.

The use of the phrase *The Lion Grip* is peculiarly significant, as Major Sanderson shows in his work, *An Examination of the Masonic Ritual*. Therein he points out that in the *Book of the Dead* the Supreme God, whether Ra or Osiris, is appealed to as the " God in the Lion form," and in all such cases the prayer of the Soul is that he may be permitted to " Come forth " in the East, rising with the sun from the d...s of the g.. In Egypt the lion was the 'personification of strength and power, but it is usually associated with the idea of the regeneration of the Sun, and therefore with the resurrection. Major Sanderson goes on to point out as follows. " Shu (*Anheru*, ' the Lifter ') who as the light of the Dawn was said to lift up the sky-goddess from the arms of the sleeping Earth, is often represented as a lion, for only through him was the rebirth of the Sun made possible. Osiris is called the lion of yesterday, and Ra the Lion of to-morrow : the bier of Osiris is always represented as having the head and legs of a lion." Thus as Major Sanderson indicates, the expression "the lion grip" is a survival from the Solar cult, and therefore a landmark which should be carefully preserved.

The Bright Morning Star whose rising brings peace and Salvation, almost certainly was originally Sirius, but to Englishmen it must seem strange that Sirius should be said to bring peace and Salvation. The association of these ideas with the Dog Star is undoubtedly a fragment which has come down from Ancient Egypt, for the rising of Sirius marked the beginning of the inundation of the Nile, which literally brought salvation to the people of Egypt by irrigating the land and enabling it to produce food. That Sirius was an object of veneration to the philosophers of the ancient world is well known to all archaeologists, and many of the Temples in Egypt have been proved to have been oriented on Sirius. There is also a good deal of evidence showing that some of the stone circles in Great Britain were similarly oriented on Sirius by the Druids. It is therefore not surprising that this star is still remembered in our rituals. Naturally it has acquired a deeper spiritual meaning in the course of years, and may be regarded as representing the First Fruits of the Resurrection, the sure hope of our

Redemption. This aspect is set forth in the lectures drawn up by Dunckerley, who regarded it as the star of Bethlehem, and as typifying Christ. See Rev. xxii, 16.

At this point the Can., who has been carefully put in the N., the place of darkness, is moved round by the right to the South. From the practical point of view this is to enable the M. to re-enter his chair from the proper side, but there is also an inner meaning. Immediately after death the Soul is said to find itself on the earth plane amid murk and darkness. Lacking mortal eyes, it cannot perceive the sun, and, on the other hand, is still so immersed in matter that it cannot yet see clearly with its spirit eyes ; but this stage rapidly passes away, and the Soul is received into a higher plane of existence, being brought thither by messengers of Light. The position in the North represents this period of darkness on the earth plane, and that this is not accidental is shown by the fact that in most rituals the lights are not turned up until the phrase " That bright morning star, etc." has been uttered. Then the M., representing one of these spirit messengers, leads the Can. gently round to the South, thereby symbolising his entry into the place of light. And who is this messenger ?   Every installed master who has received the P.W. *leading* to the Chair should realise that, no matter how unworthy, he represents the risen Christ.   Thus we see the peculiarly appropriate nature of the act coming after the reference to the bright morning star, which also in another sense represents the risen Christ.

CHAPTER V

THE S....TS

Having thus been brought into the place of light, the Can. is given not the Gen. S.s, but only substituted ones. This fact must often have puzzled the Can.. The practical reason given in the ritual, though perfectly intelligible to a R.A. mason, cannot be the real one. In view of the unexpected calamity no-one could have thought K.S. was breaking his ob. by nominating a successor to H.A.B. and giving him the full s....ts. Actually, according to the R.A. story, he did something much worse, for he wrote them down and placed them somewhere, in the hopes that they would be subsequently rediscovered, and he had no assurance that their discoverers would even be masons, much less that they would keep their discovery secret. Of course this is also an allegory, and from this standpoint perfectly correct. The lost s....ts are the nature and attributes of God, which must be realised by each man for himself, and no other man can really communicate them. Moreover, this complete realisation of the nature of God, and the union of the Divine Spark within us with the Source of All, can never be achieved during mortal life. Even after death we shall need to leave the world long behind and travel far, before we can hope to attain that state of spiritual evolution which will enable us to approach the Holy of Holies, and gaze with unveiled eyes upon Him, Who is the beginning and the end of all.

With regard to these substituted s....ts. let us note that they grow out of those used by the F.C. . Having already shown in the last book that the sn.s of the F.C., and in fact the real s...t of that degree, is the transformation of *Jehovah* into *Jeheshue*, we see that this is most appropriate. To use modern language, the second degree teaches of the birth of the Christ Spirit within us, while the third indicates that mystically we, like the great Master, must die and rise again. As St. Paul says, " Die daily in Christ."

The sn.s given are probably all of great antiquity. Of some we have evidence which shows that they were venerated in ancient Egypt and Mexico, are still employed in the primitive Initiatory Rites of the savages, and are associated with the Gods in India. For example, the P.S. is used by Shiva, the Great Destroyer, Who when He makes it, holds in His hand the lariet of death. The sn. of G. and D. is found all round the world, as I have shown in full detail in *Sign Language of the Ancient Mysteries*. Ancient Mexico, where Quetzacoatl makes it, can be matched with Easter Island in the far Pacific, Peru, West Africa, East Africa, New Guinea, Malaya and many other places.

Major Sanderson points out that the second Cas. Sn. is depicted in Egyptian pictures as being used by those who are saluting Osiris in his coffin. Those who desire will find it in Papyrus 9,908 in the British Museum.

The English sn. of g. and d. (for up till now we have been speaking of the Scotch form) is almost certainly not the correct one. Its general appearance would incline one to believe that it is a penal sn., though whence derived it is difficult to say. A little thought will indicate the nature of the penalty as being somewhat similar to that of one of the higher degrees. So far as I can find it is not recognised as a sn. of g. and d. to-day, except among

masons who are descended masonically from the
Grand Lodge of England, but in a picture by Guer-
cino of Christ cleansing the Temple, in the *Palazzo
Rosso*, Genoa, both this and the Scotch form are
shown, while the G. of H. constantly appears in
mediaeval paintings, e.g., in the Raising of Lazarus.[1]

The so-called Continental form undoubtedly
comes from a well known high degree, where it is
much more appropriate : it is apparently restricted
to the Latin countries, whereas even in Germany it
is the Scotch form that is employed.

The sn. of Exul. is a form used to this day in
most parts of Asia to indicate worship, and was
similarly employed in Ancient Egypt. Major Sanderson suggests that it was copied from the position in
which Shu upheld the sky.

Thus we see that six out of the so-called seven
sn.s can be shown to be of ancient origin, and it is
quite probable that further research will enable
us to prove that the other one is equally old. Such
sn.s as these originally had a magical significance,
and the explanation given in the ritual as to their

---

[1] See *The Sign Language of the Mysteries* by Ward.

origin is no doubt of a much later date than the sn.s themselves. Indeed, a careful study of certain of the sn.s will show that they are not the natural sn.s which would have been used to indicate the feeling they are said to express. For example, ιn the sn. of h.......r the left hand would not naturally be placed in the position in which we are taught to put it, if this sn. had originated as related in the story. So obvious is this that some modern preceptors of Lodges of Instruction have to my knowledge altered the position of the left hand in order to make it conform to the story, but I venture to think that in so doing they are committing a very serious mistake, nothing less than the removal of an ancient landmark.

Some day we shall probably discover the real origin of this sn., but if it is altered that will of course become impossible.

The lion's grip and the actual position of r...s...g are equally old, and, so far as we can find, this manner of r...s.:.g is employed in every rite, whether ancient or primitive, which deals with the dramatic representation of d.... As a manner of greeting it is employed by the initiated men in many Red

Indian Tribes, in West Africa, among the Senussi
in North Africa, and in the Dervish Rites.[1]

The parts of the b. brought in contact with each
other are all parts presided over by some sign of
the Zodiac, and there would appear to be some
old astrological meaning which has now become
lost. It may possibly have been connected with
Gemini, the Twins, and this fact is made the more
probable by the survival of the name " The Ln's
Gr." The explanation given, although possibly
of a fairly recent origin, nevertheless contains a
valuable inner meaning, for it shows that we cannot hope to advance towards God unless we do
our duty to our fellow men. Thus in dramatic
form is shown that the brotherhood of man neces-
sitates the Fatherhood of God.

It hardly seems necessary in this book to point
out again that the regular st. forms a tau cross
and teaches us that we must trample under foot
our animal passions, if we desire to approach near
to God. We note, however, that the Can., in advancing to obtain the s...ts, has perforce to make
three tau crosses, and the Christian Mystic will

[1] For further explanation see Ward, *Who Was Hiram Abiff?*

doubtless perceive in this a hidden reference to the three crosses on Calvary.

Finally, as has already been pointed out, the penalties of the first and second degrees draw attention to two important occult centres, and so also in this degree the Solar Plexus, the most important occult centre of all, is indicated, and since the object of every Mystic is to achieve the Beatific vision, the fact that the monks of Mt. Athos, near Salonica, do so by fixing their eye on this part, shows that there is a very special reason for the special form of the p.s of the third degree.

CHAPTER VI

THE BADGE

On his re-entering the Lodge the Can. is presented, and in due course invested by the S.W., as in the previous degrees, thereby indicating that even after death man's spiritual advancement is registered by the Soul. The Badge itself, however, is full of symbolic meaning, and though in its present form it is of comparatively recent date, it is evident that those who designed it had a much deeper knowledge of symbolism than some modern critics are apt to believe.

Firstly, the colour, which is that of Cambridge University, and likewise that used by Parliament when fighting King Charles, has a much deeper significance than is generally known. It is closely related to the colour of the Virgin Mary, which itself had been brought forward from Isis and the other Mother Goddesses of the ancient world. It is possible that the designers were also influenced by the existence of certain Orders of Knighthood which had their appropriate colours, for the aprons of Grand Lodge Officers have Garter blue, but this blue is also the colour of Oxford, and the colour associated with the Royalist cause at the time of the Civil War. At any rate, it is appropriate that our aprons should thus employ the colours of the two great Universities of England. There is, of course, an exception in the case of the red aprons allocated to Grand Stewards, for which there are historical reasons into which we need not now enter. We may, however, point out that the dark blue aprons of Grand Lodge are often, though erroneously, spoken of as the Purple, indicating a Royal colour, and thereby implying no doubt that Brn. entitled to wear this colour are rulers in the Craft, and represent the masculine element. Light blue, on the other hand, represents the feminine or passive aspect, and is most appropriate for the ordinary M.M., whose duty it is to obey, and not to command. Indeed, the M.M.'s apron contains other emblems which indicate this feminine aspect. These are the three rosettes, which symbolise the rose, itself a substitute for the Vesica Piscis, and they are arranged so as to form a triangle with the point upwards, interpenetrating the triangle formed by the flap of the apron. The two triangles only interpenetrate half way, therein differing from the double triangles seen on the jewels worn by R. A. Masons, which completely overlap. These two triangles deserve a little careful study. The lower triangle with its point upwards is the triangle of fire, the emblem of Shiva, and the symbol of the Divine Spark. The triangle made by the flap of the apron, which has its point directed downwards, is the triangle of water, and is thus to some extent representative of the Soul. These two triangles are within a sq., the emblem of matter, and therefore of the body, and so we see that the M.M.'s apron symbolically represents the triune nature of man, whereas the R.A. jewel, (the only high degree jewel which may be worn in a Craft Lodge) has these two triangles within a circle, which is the emblem of the Infinite. In this case the triangle of water presents the preservative aspect, the triangle of fire, the destructive aspect, the point or eye at the centre, the creative aspect, and the circle, the everlasting nature of the Supreme Being. There is therefore a curious correspondence, and also a marked difference, between the jewel of the R.A. Mason, and the apron of the M.M. .

Viewed from another standpoint the apron has another set of meanings. The triangle represents Spirit, and the Sq., matter. The flap forms a triangle entering into the sq., and so depicts the entry of Spirit into matter, and therefore, man. The E.A.'s apron should have the flap pointing upward, indicating that the Divine Wisdom has not yet truly penetrated the gross matter of our bodies. This custom is unfortunately going out of use in modern Masonry, which is a great pity, as undoubtedly a valuable lesson is thus lost. The F.C. has the flap pointing downward for several reasons. Firstly, to indicate that wisdom has begun to enter and therefore to control matter; secondly, to represent the triangle of water and thus indicate that Soul and Body are acting in unison; thirdly, because this triangle is the emblem of Vishnu the Preserver, and so emphasises the fact that the aspect of God taught in this degree is the preservative aspect, whereas the addition of the three rosettes in the third degree shows, not only the union of Body, Soul and *Spirit*, but also that the great lesson of this degree is the importance of the Destructive side of the Diety, or as we may prefer to call it, the Transformative side.

What, however, of the two rosettes worn by the F.C.? Firstly, they stress the dual nature of man, and have a very clear reference to the two p........rs. Similarly, no doubt, they indicate that the F.C. is not yet a complete and united being; Body and Soul are in union, but unlike the M.M., these two are not in complete accord with the Spirit. Thus we obtain a correspondence between the knocks of the F.C. and the two rosettes. Furthermore, the triangle is incomplete, showing that the F.C. is not yet a complete F.M., and this correlates with the position of the C.s when taking the ob. in the F.C. degree.

Two other features of the apron must also be considered. Firstly, the tassels, which appear originally to have been the ends of the string with which the apron was bound round the waist. There is little doubt that in the 18th century the aprons had not the present symbolic tassels, but were fastened round the body in a very similar way to that in which the E.A. and F.C. aprons are to this day. It is interesting to note in this connection that the actual aprons worn by the officers of Grand Lodge for the year, as distinct from the Past Grand Officers' aprons, have no tassels at all.

In the course of years, no doubt, the ends of the strings were ornamented by tassels, and to this day the aprons of the Royal Order of Scotland are bound round the body by an ornamental cord with tassels, which are tied in front in such a way that the two tassels stick out from underneath the flap. These tassels, when the final form of our aprons was fixed, were separated from the bands which fasten the apron, and attached to the apron itself, becoming as we now see simply strips of ribbon on which are fastened seven chains. When this change took place it is clear that those who made the alteration deliberately chose the number 7, and intended thereby to convey a symbolic meaning. We have already explained the numerous symbolic meanings of the number 7; for example, it represents God and Man, Spirit and Matter, etc.

Naturally they had to have two tassels to balance, and it would have been very inartistic to have had four chains on one tassel and three on the other, and so it would be unwise to lay too much stress on the number 14, which is the sum total. We may regard it merely as a curious and interesting coincidence that the body of Osiris was stated to have been divided by Set into 14 pieces. But in addition to these details as to the historical development of the tassels, we must not forget that in many of the 18th

Century aprons the two p....rs are depicted. These aprons were usually decorated by paintings on the leather, and varied considerably from Lodge to Lodge, but one of the most usual kinds of decoration included the two p....rs, and the remembrance of these may very probably have influenced those who designed our present apron.

The modern arrangement by which the apron is fastened, namely, a piece of webbing with a hook and eye attachment, gave a fine opportunity for some really profound symbolism, and I feel certain that it was not an accident which led to the universal adoption of the snake to serve this purpose.

There are two kinds of symbolism attached to the snake in all ancient religions. Firstly, the snake as the enemy of man, and therefore as the representative of the powers of evil ; and secondly the snake as emblem of the Divine Wisdom. " Be ye wise as serpents " does not refer to the craftiness of the Devil, but to the Divine Wisdom itself. In Ancient Egypt the Soul as he passed through the Underworld met with serpents of evil, and also with serpents of good. In India, legend tells us of a whole order of beings, the Serpent Folk, who *are* of a Spiritual nature different from man, possessed their own rulers, and were endowed with superhuman wisdom. Some of these *are* considered to be friendly to man, while others *are* hostile. The Sacred Cobra is well known to every student of Hindu religions, and is essentially good. Actual worship is paid to the Serpent throughout the whole of India, and in many other parts of the world, and in the Kapala we get clear traces of the fact that under certain circumstances the serpent is regarded as " The Shining One " — the Holy Wisdom Itself. Thus we see that the serpent on our apron denotes that we are encircled by the Holy Wisdom.

Finally, the serpent biting its tail, and thus forming a circle, has always been regarded as the emblem of eternity, and more especially of the Eternal Wisdom of God. Nor must we forget that the snake is peculiarly associated with Shiva, whose close symbolic association with the third degree has already been clearly shown.

Much more might be written on the meaning of the apron, but we cannot devote any more space to this subject, interesting though it may be, although before considering our next point it will perhaps be well to recall what has already been mentioned in the E.A. Handbook, viz., that aprons, in addition to their Operative significance, have right through the ages been employed in connection with religious ceremonial. On the monuments of Egypt a garment, which can best be described as a triangular apron with the point upward, is depicted in circumstances indicating that the wearer is taking part in some kind of ceremony of initiation. In ancient Mexico the Gods are depicted wearing aprons, and it is not without interest to note that the modern Anglican bishop wears an apron, although it appears to have developed from a long flowing robe somewhat the shape of a cassock.

CHAPTER VII

THE LEGEND

After the ceremonial investiture of the Cand. the
W.M. continues the narrative of the traditional
history. At least this is the case in most English
workings, but in some Scotch workings the whole
story is told first, and subsequently the Cand. and
the other Brn. act the chief parts. Perhaps one of
the most important points to realise is the correct
meaning of the name H.A.B. . Major Sanderson in
An Examination of the Masonry Ritual gives the
following interesting interpretations, which we will
proceed to expand further.—" The title H.A.B. is
taken direct from the Hebrew of 2 Chron., Chapter
4, verse 16., and means, ' H. His father.' H. means
' Exaltation of light, their liberty or whiteness, he
that destroys ' ; It is of interest to note that *abib*
in Hebrew means ' Ears of corn,' or ' Green fruits,'
and there is just a possibility that this is the correct
title of H."

Bearing these translations in mind we at once
perceive a whole series of inner meanings hidden

in the name of the principal Architect. Taking the Christian interpretation of our rituals :—firstly, we shall remember that Christ said " If I am raised up (or exalted) I shall draw all men unto me." Secondly, Christ died to make us free, that is, to give us liberty from the bonds of death and hell. Thirdly, mediaeval divines were never tired of referring to Christ's whiteness and purity, and relate many beautiful legends and allegories to drive home this lesson. One phrase alone will suffice to bring this aspect of the Christ to our minds, i.e., that He is constantly spoken of as " the lily of the valley." Fourthly, He came to destroy the bonds of death and hell, nor must we forget the old prophecy spoken concerning the coming Christ and the serpent, representing Satan, " It (Christ) shall bruise thy head, and thou shalt bruise His heel," Gen. 3. v. 15. It is of interest to note that Quetzacoatl, the Mexican Preserver, who fought and overthrew the great giant of evil, was himself smitten in the foot, near to a fall of water, subsequently died from the wound, and ultimately rose again from the grave. In India Krishna similarly died from an arrow wound in the heel. Moreover, in mediaeval frescoes Christ is constantly represented as crushing the head of the great dragon under His left foot, while in His right hand He upraises a staff on which is a cross. Such scenes are usually described as " The Harrowing of Hell."

Fifthly, if the word *abib* is the correct rendering for the second half of the name in question, we get a clear reference to the Sacramental bread. The ears of corn are obviously synonymous with the wafer, or consecrated bread, which in mediaeval days alone was given to the laity : while the alternative translation, " Green Fruits," brings to our mind the Biblical saying that Christ is " the first fruits of them that slept " (1 Corin, 15. 20). Bearing this possible Christian interpretation in mind, in-stalled masters will perceive the deep significance of the P.W. which leads from the degree of M.M. to that of I.M.

But in addition to these Christian interpretations of H.A.B. there is yet another, which in some senses may be regarded as older, and the key to which is supplied by India. In this sense H.A.B. takes on the characteristics of Shiva, the Destroyer.

Firstly, " Exaltation of life " reminds us of the legend that Shiva on a certain day increased in stature until He overtopped the universe, and, as a result, overthrew Brahma, the Creator, and was acknowledged by Vishnu as His superior. On that great day He gathered unto Himself the beginning and the end of all things, Alpha and Omega, and henceforth birth and death alike were in His hands.

Secondly, " Their liberty " refers to the fact that, to the pious Hindu, Shiva by death grants liberty from the toil and anguish of this world, and sets the soul free to mount to greater heights of spirituality.

Thirdly, Shiva is always spoken of as the " Great White God, white with the ashes of the dead who are ever burned in His honour." Nor must we forget that these ashes are always scattered to the four cardinal points of Heaven.

Fourthly, He is in His very essence " The Great Destroyer."

The " Ears of corn " are symbols of Vishnu the Preserver, Who Himself, according to numerous Hindu legends, was slain and rose from the dead, thereby paying allegiance to the Lord of Death ; and so :

Fifthly, we obtain the idea of the Resurrection as symbolised by the ears of corn, which are planted in the earth and bring forth an abundant harvest, the " Green fruits " of the fields. In this connection it is as well to remember that the central theme of the Eleusinian Mysteries was the ear of corn which was shown to the Cand. at the most solemn point of the whole ceremony, and similarly taught the doctrine of the resurrection from the dead.

The next point that strikes us in the legend is the number of craftsmen who " went in search." The Irish version is of peculiar interest, for it relates that it was the twelve who relented who afterwards " went in search," and not a new company of fifteen. In many ways this is more logical, and certainly has a deep symbolic meaning. It is logical in that it shows that the penitent twelve did their best to make amends for ever having allowed themselves to listen to the wicked schemes of the other three, and the subsequent decree of K.S., ordering them to wear white gloves and white aprons as a mark of their innocence, is most appropriate. It was a public announcement that K.S. forgave them their indiscretion and acquitted them of responsibility for the crime.

On the other hand, in our version there seems no logical reason why K.S. should order an entirely new batch of F.C.'s to wear these emblems of their innocence, since they clearly had nothing to do with the crime, and moreover, all the others, except the penitent twelve, were equally innocent, and should therefore likewise have been instructed to wear white gloves and aprons. It must be remembered that these white gloves, etc., were not bestowed as a reward for having taken part in the search, but are specifically stated to have been ordered to be worn to denote innocence.

The Irish account goes on to state that the twelve set out from the Temple and went together in one company until they came to a place where four roads met, and formed a cross; then they divided into four companies, and three went North, three East, three South, and three West. Thus they trod the Way of the Cross. In some old Irish workings we are told that the three who went North never returned. This symbolically implies that they went into the Place of Darkness. As the tendency in modern Irish masonry appears to be to adjust its ritual in main essentials to our English workings, it is but fair that I should say that I have a tangible proof of this form of legend, in the shape of an old Irish apron dated 1790, which, unlike modern Irish aprons, has a number of paintings on it depicting incidents in the ritual. One of the paintings shows the twelve F.C.'s separating at the four cross roads. (See frontispiece).

It is clear from all accounts, whether English, Irish, Scotch or American, that the scoundrels, the agents of death, were found by those who went in the direction of Joppa, that is in the W., but we are left in considerable doubt as to whether the b. was found in the E. or in the S.. Symbolically, however, it would clearly be in the S., for H.A.B., like the Christ, was struck down at High Twelve, when the sun is in the S.. From a practical point of view it is fairly obvious that the scoundrels who were carrying away the b. could never have reached Joppa if they had once gone E., for they would have had to fetch half a circle round Jerusalem, a procedure which would have rendered their chance of escape almost hopeless. By going S. they might hope to throw their pursuers off the track, and then turn back at an angle, reach Joppa, and escape by boat. That this was their intention is clear from many old forms of the legend, and especially in those worked in America. King S., however, fore-saw this possibility and prevented their escape by forbidding any ships to sail. In the American working one of the officers of the Lodge enacts the part of a sea captain, and even wears a yachtman's cap. The villains come to him and beg him to take them aboard, but he refused because of the embargo ordered by K.S.. That the same incident was known in the old Irish working is shown by the little picture on the same Irish apron depicting the arrest of the villains on the sea shore, for in the back ground there is a ship.

Let us interpret the meaning of the Irish work-ing first. From the Christian standpoint the twelve F.C.'s represent the twelve apostles, Matthias re-placing the traitor Judas. But in the non-Christian, and possibly earlier interpretation, these twelve would of course be the twelve signs of the Zodiac, searching for the sun which had been eclipsed. We must never forget that in addition to the deep spiritual meaning hidden in our ritual there is also a Solar Myth embedded, which has in the course of years become allegorized and filled with deeper spiritual truths.

But being English masons we must be prepared to find an explanation of the fifteen. In ancient Egyptian times the month consisted of 30 days, and the year of twelve such months, plus five extra days. Now the first fifteen, of whom twelve recanted, presumably represent the first half of that month, while the second half of the month is represented by the fifteen who went in search. But spiritually the meaning of the fifteen is fairly clear. Man has five senses and is triune in nature, and this implies that Body, Soul and Spirit must co-operate in trying to find God, and employ on that quest their five senses.

Lest there be any misapprehension here I would explain that man is considered to have not only the five physical senses, but also corresponding senses of Soul and Spirit. The phrase " To see with the eyes of the Spirit " is perfectly well known, and similarly we can speak of the eyes of the Soul. To give concrete examples :—Students of psychic science constantly speak of clairaudience and clairvoyance. While it is not necessary to accept this type of phenomena, it is clearly obvious that if man survives death at all his Soul must have a means of communicating with other Souls, and that these correspond in some way to our physical senses. In like manner how are we to describe the visions of the great seers and prophets, related in the Bible, except by the possession of spiritual sight ?

Bearing this in mind, we obtain the following interpretation of the fate which befell the three F.C. Lodges into which the fifteen formed themselves. Those who found nothing represent the physical senses of man, which are useless beyond the grave : the next company must therefore represent the Soul, for despite the logic of the physical world, it is the Soul which realises that death does not end all, and so it was one of these who r....d the M.... But the power which tells us what is right and wrong, and which ultimately punishes us for our offences, is what we call conscience, and this assuredly is the Divine Spark within us—the Spirit.

Let us now turn to consider the details connected with the discovery of the body. The incident of the shrub is such a striking analogy with a similar one found in Æneid, wherein Æneas finds the body of the murdered Polydorus by plucking up a shrub which is near him on the side of a hill, that some students suggest that in the revision of our ritual this incident was copied from Virgil. But, in *Who was Hiram Abiff*, I show that both refer back to an ancient source and have an allegorical meaning. One proof supporting this view is that this particular tree, the Acacia, has from time immemorial been more or less sacred in the near East. In ancient Egypt the earliest forms of the legend of Osiris relate that it was an acacia which grew up round the coffin of Osiris, and not a tamarisk as in the later versions. (See *An Examination of the Masonic Ritual*, by Major Sanderson). In like manner this tree is sacred in Arabia, India, and many parts of Africa, while it is the Shittim wood of the Old Testament, from which the ark was made. No doubt in this reverence for the acacia we have a survival of the primitive veneration for trees, usually spoken of as " tree and serpent worship." In India the assouata tree is stated to be a symbol of Trimurti, the Three in One. Its roots represent Brahma, its trunk Vishnu, and its branches Shiva, the Destroyer.

At any rate we can regard the acacia tree as in itself an emblem of the resurrection, for the tiny seed which is buried brings forth a mighty tree, covered with fragrant blossoms.

The account of the manner in which the Cas. S....s came into existence, though ingenious, can hardly be taken as historic. As we have already dealt with this point previously, we shall only say that every folk-lore student is well aware that, in the vast majority of cases, legends purporting to explain the origin of a certain custom do not give the real origin at all, but merely indicate that the origin of the custom has been lost, owing to its great antiquity. The very manner in which some of the S....s are given is sufficient to indicate that they did not originate in the way suggested, while, on the other hand, we find these same S....s all round the world, with entirely different explanations as to their origin. They are indeed ancient landmarks, and the utmost care should be taken not to alter them in any way.

The next incident in the legend is the capture of the scoundrels. In some rituals it is given with much interesting detail of a picturesque nature. All agree that they were apprehended in a cavern, and many say explicitly that it was near the sea shore. Some of the rituals state that the fugitives were overheard lamenting as follows :—" One said, ' Oh, that my t. had been c.a. rather than I should have done it;' while another more sorrowfully exclaimed, 'Oh, that my h........t had been t.o. rather than that I should have struck him;' and a third voice brokenly said, 'Oh, that my b. had been s. in t. rather than that I should have smitten him.'" This last version is of interest as explaining the legendary origin of the py. of the three degrees, and incidentally it shows how legend incorporates facts into a story, in order to explain something whose original meaning is lost. It would also appear from this version as if the scoundrels had not intended to actually kill their victim but merely to terrorise him, and in the excitement of the moment lost their heads. Symbolically this contains a valuable piece of teaching. According to one interpretation the three scoundrels represent "The lust of the flesh, and the lust of the eyes, and the pride of life" (1 John, 2. 16). In other words, the sins of the flesh, the sins of the Soul, such as covetousness, and spiritual pride, the most deadly of all.

These sins assuredly destroy man both physically and spiritually, yet it can truly be said that in giving way to them no man intends to destroy himself. From the more strictly Christian standpoint the three scoundrels are Herod, Caiaphas, and

Pontius Pilate, and it is perfectly clear that Pilate and Herod, at any rate, did not wish to kill our Lord, but were caught in a position from which they found it impossible to escape.

Returning to the deeper mystical interpretation we notice that the scoundrels were found in the West, the region of Death, which teaches us that the just retribution for all our sins, whether of body, soul, or spirit, will overtake us after death, and that though in one sense it is God, here shadowed forth by K.S., who punishes, yet in another sense it is our five spiritual faculties which themselves rise up in judgment against us. We ourselves, doom ourselves, and therefore we can obtain nothing but strict justice.

Without pretending that we have exhausted this subject, this brief explanation of the true character of the scoundrels and their captors must suffice, and we will only mention in passing that here also there appears to be a half forgotten astrological reference to the three winter months which oppress the sun.

CHAPTER VIII

THE TRACING BOARD, ETC.

The next part of the narrative is incorporated in most English workings with the Tracing Board. The most interesting feature is the description of the g.. It is obvious that peculiar stress is laid on the centre, even in the present form of our ritual, because of the way in which the measurements are given. Why should it not have been said that it was six feet long? In some old rituals the g., or rather the monument, is described as a dome, which made a complete circle at its base, and was three feet from the centre every way. If so it must have been like a small replica of the earliest form of the Buddhist Pagoda, and the Master was thus buried at the centre. In that case the top of the dome would have been five feet from the surface of the ground, and we should thus get the correct symbolic use of 5 as representing the body, and 3 as representing the spirit, while enabling the human body to be decorously interred. It seems probably that when the g. was made to conform to the type familiar in England, a desperate effort was made to retain the 3 and 5. It is worth noting that there is no mention of the use of any c...f......n, despite the picture on the tracing board, and if a c...f......n had been used at the supposed date of the incident it certainly would not have been of the European shape depicted, but much more like an Egyptian Sarcophagus. Nevertheless, though the ritual does not justify the existence of any c...f......n on the tracing board, it was an integral part of the ancient mysteries of Osiris, and its retention in our ritual is almost certainly an ancient landmark. On the same tracing board may be seen certain letters in the Masonic cypher, which are practically never explained. Very often when transliterated, among other things, they will be found to give the P.W. leading to the three degree. This fact is of interest, for the true meaning of that W., as already explained, is a w...k...r in m......ls, the correct description of H.A.B. The fact that he was buried as near the Sanctum Sanctorum as possible, symbolically denotes that he had reached the centre, and was in union with the Source of All.

The Dormer window historically is the hypostyle, the method by which Egyptian and classical temples obtained light. The pillars of the central nave of such temples rose considerably higher than the roofs of the aisles, thus leaving openings through which the light could enter the building. These, however, were many in number, and it is difficult to justify the apparent statement that there was only one such opening. Symbolically it is intended to represent the means by which the Divine Light penetrates into the deepest recesses of every man's nature.

The squared pavement has already been explained under the section dealing with the mosaic pavement, in the first degree, and our readers are therefore referred to it. Briefly, it indicates that man's progress towards the centre is through alternate experiences of good and evil, darkness and light, mercy and severity, life and death.

The Porch which is the entrance to the Sanctum Sanctorum is the gateway of death.

The working tools, as in other cases, contain much sound moral teaching of typical 18th Century work, but there is one implement which deserves rather more than passing attention. For what follows I must express my indebtedness to W. Bro. Sir John Cockburn, P.G.D. The s....k....t does not appear to be much in use among Operative masons. It *is* used by gardeners, but the Operative mason has other means for marking out the ground for the foundations. This implement has more than a superficial resemblance to the Caduceus of Mercury, and Sir John Cockburn suggests that it has been employed to replace this " Heathen " emblem. For my part, I think this is most probable, for it is clear that at the beginning of the 19th century a deliberate attempt was made to eliminate this emblem from our ceremonies. The jewel of the Deacons in the 18th century was not a dove, but a figure of Mercury, bearing the Caduceus. A number of these old jewels can be seen in the library of Grand Lodge, and there are still a few old Lodges which continue to use them, instead of the modern jewel. Now this jewel is far more appropriate to the Deacons than is a dove. A dove is the emblem of peace, and a carrier pigeon bears messages, but neither of these birds do all the work of the Deacons. Mercury, however, was the Messenger of the Gods, and carried the instructions of Jupiter, thus fulfilling one set of the duties of a deacon. He was also the conductor of souls through the underworld ; taking the dead by one hand, and uplifting the Caduceus in the other, he led the Shade from the grave, through the perils of the underworld, to the Elysian Fields; before his Caduceus the powers of evil fled. In mediaeval escatology it is *Christ* who leads the Souls on a similar journey, uplifting in His Hand the Cross of Salvation. Even to-day the jewels of the Deacons in a Mark Lodge bear the Caduceus, a mute but convincing witness to the use of this emblem in Freemasonry.

We can thus see that on the one hand a deliberate effort was made to delete from our ceremonies the Caduceus, probably because it was considered to be Pagan, while on the other hand it was clearly quite easy for ignorant masonic furnishers, in the course of years, to make the Caduceus approximate more and more to a masonic tool, so as to fit it in with other avowedly masonic implements. As a masonic tool it has very little significance, even to a Speculative, and is of no practical value to an Operative, but the Caduceus would be peculiarly appropriate to the third degree. In short, it is an ancient landmark, an emblem of the dead and forgotten Mysteries, and symbolical of Him who leads the soul from the darkness of the grave to the light of the resurrection.

Before leaving the M.M. degree let me say to all installed masters that *if* they have received the P.W., not the W. of an Installed master, but the *P.W.* leading from the M.M. to that further degree, they will find in it evidence not of a mere hint of the resurrection, but of the Resurrection itself, and a close association with the version of that doctrine set forth in the life of the Perfect Master.

CHAPTER IX

THE CLOSING

Here we are reminded that we are working in symbolism, for we come back from the West, i.e., the grave, to this material world. But we have only obtained substitutes, and we offer them as some consolation to the spirit, i.e., the W.M. The advance to the centre of the room is an obvious reference to the other centre. The s......s are communicated by the body to the soul, which passes them on to the spirit. The meaning of these s.......s is dealt with in the ceremony, but it is worth noting that the word shows clearly that the s.......t is to be found only through the death of the body. The actual Hebrew word whose corrupt form we use really means " My son is slain." It is also well to remember that the p.s. and the s. of G. & D. (Scottish form) are old signs which come down from the ancient mysteries, and are still found throughout the world. A brief summary of what has already been said may be helpful. The p.s. is often associated with Shiva, the Destroyer, and is also found appropriately used at Burobudor in Java; it refers to that occult centre, the solar plexus. In view of what the lost s....t is, this sign is therefore most significant. In other words, it is a hint to those who deserve to know while it conceals from those who do not.

The Scottish sign of G. & D. is found all round the world, and always has the same meaning of an appeal for help. It is used in the most primitive initiatory rites of a boy into manhood, and in Kenya the boy makes it to indicate that he is ready for the operation of circumcision to begin. In Nyasaland, among the Yaos, it is associated with a grave, and in Mexico the Preserver is shown making it. He was slain and rose from the dead, and it is constantly found in Mexico in the form of a carving, consisting of a skeleton cut in half at the centre and making this sign, as, for example, at the Temple of Uxmal.

The manner of communicating the s.......s and the gr. are equally old. Indeed, the lion's grip appears to be the grip of all the Mysteries. It was the Grip of Mithra, and by this grip Osiris was raised. Among the Druids it was also known, as is shown by a carving at Iona. I have, however, gone into the evidence for the antiquity of our signs so fully that I will not take up further space here.

We may as well add, however, that the number " 5 " no doubt refers to the five senses of man, just as the seven steps remind us of the Egyptian sub-division of every mortal.

Having received the sub. s........s the W.M., or Spirit, confirms their use till the true ones are discovered. This last remark indicates that the quest is not ended or abandoned, in reality it has just begun ; the first stage only has been passed, which stage is death. It also tells every Craft mason that he cannot be a good craftsman till he has at least taken the Royal Arch.

Thus the spirit acknowledges that death is a step forward. It has freed the soul of the trammels imposed on it by the body, and so our life's work on earth, as symbolised in the Lodge, is closed. The knocks indicate that the spirit now dominates the soul and body, and before we leave these heights it is well to point out that almost all the great religious teachers have taught that in some mysterious way this physical body will be transformed, and still be used after death. In short, that matter, as well as spirit, is part of God. Science has shown that matter is indestructable, though its form may be changed completely, and so even after the symbolical death and resurrection, three knocks are still required.

CHAPTER X

CONCLUSION

This then concludes the third degree. More than any other degree in Craft Masonry it has embedded in it ancient landmarks, brought down from a long distant past. Under the surface lie hidden, meanings within meanings, which I make no pretence to have exhausted. Already this book has exceeded in length either of the two previous ones, but to do full justice to the sublime degree one would require a volume four times as large as this. I trust, however, that I have given some help, more especially to younger brethren, which will aid them to glimpse the deeper side of Freemasonry. If they too will strive to discover further alternative meanings, I shall feel this labour of mine has been well repaid.

Let me again warn them that just because Masonry is so old, its rituals, in the course of years, have been again and again revised, and newer meanings have continually been grafted on to the old stock.

We are not entitled to say one meaning is right and another wrong. Both may be right. Christianity itself has taken over a vast mass of pre-Christian ceremonies and symbols, and the student is perfectly entitled to consider that both the Christian and the pre-Christian interpretations of these symbols are equally deserving of respect.

There is also another point which should be borne in mind. Again and again we find that incidents and phrases which appear to have come from the Bible, on closer investigation are found not to correspond exactly with the Biblical narrative. At one time there was a tendency to say that in these cases it was our duty to substitute the Biblical version for the "Inaccurate" traditional form. With all due respect I venture to say that such action is totally unjustifiable. Masonry is not the Bible. It is a traditional ritual into which 18th century revisers inserted fragments from the Bible, because that was the only book dealing with the period of the masonic incidents which was then available to them. To-day, we know a great deal more about this period than did our 18th century predecessors, and the modern investigator has just cause to lament the well meaning, but misdirected, zeal of these worthy masons, who thereby have probably destroyed for ever valuable landmarks, which would have helped us to discover the historical growth and the symbolic meaning of many parts of our ceremonies.

Such apparent contradictions, and even mistakes, as appear to exist, should be carefully retained, for they are sure indications to the conscientous student of a connection with a long distant past, which modern methods of research may enable us finally to trace to its origin. If, however, they are revised out of existence, future generations will have nothing to help them in the task of unravelling the true history and meaning of Freemasonry.

If a Sn. does not correspond with the explanation of the manner in which it is said to have originated, don't alter the way of giving the Sn., for it is an ancient landmark. Rather try to discover if anywhere in the world that Sn. is still used in some old ceremony which may throw light on its true origin. If H.A.B. was not buried in a c...f...n, don't eliminate the c...f...n from the tracing board, but rather bear in mind that his great prototype, Osiris, *was* so buried and that the c...f...n played a peculiarly important part in the legend which recounts his death : which legend was hoary with antiquity before K.S. was born.

Finally, let me say that even if a man can never fathom the full meaning of the third degree, yet there is no man worthy of the name who has passed through that third degree but will certainly have learnt one important lesson, namely, how to d., and thereby will be the better man.

––––––––––––